GRAPHIC

1737405

Mori, Kaoru.

OCT 2 6 2008

Emma. Volume 1

Volume 1   **By Kaoru Mori**

-Contents-

Chapter 1 The Visit.....................................003

Chapter 2 The Glasses.................................029

Chapter 3 The Visitor From the East.........055

Chapter 4 The Love Letters........................081

Chapter 5 The Photograph..........................107

Chapter 6 The Two Watches.......................133

Chapter 7 The Father, Richard Jones.........159

Afterword...185

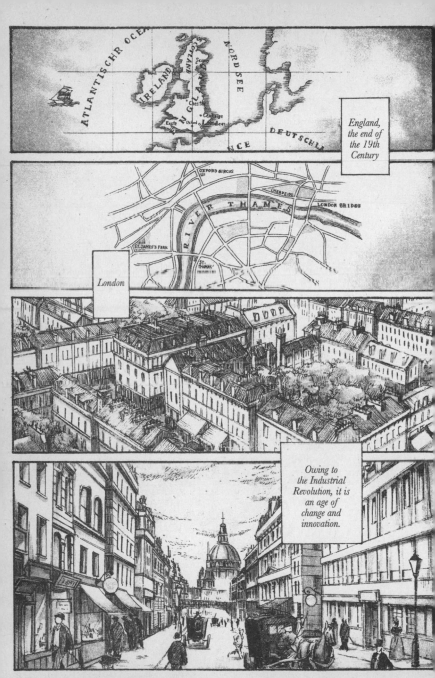

England,
the end of
the 19th
Century

London

Owing to
the Industrial
Revolution, it is
an age of
change and
innovation.

And yet...

...it is also an age when traditional lifestyles and a class system remain entrenched in society...

...and horse-drawn carriages still have the run of the road.

CHAPTER 1: THE VISITOR

I'VE MENTIONED TO YOU BEFORE, HAVEN'T I, EMMA, THAT I WAS A LIVE-IN GOVERNESS A LONG TIME AGO?

FOR THIS YOUNG MAN.

OH.

HO-HO-HO! STANDING IN FRONT OF AN OPENING DOOR. A WONDERFUL EXAMPLE OF BEING IN THE WRONG PLACE AT THE WRONG TIME!

THAT'S JUST LIKE YOU!

. . . . .

I'VE ASKED HIM TO COME OVER FOR A VISIT MANY TIMES, BUT HE NEVER HAS.

THANK YOU.

SO I'VE BEEN LEFT IN THE DARK AS TO THE STATE OF YOUR FAMILY.

AT THE TIME, THE JONES FAMILY WAS QUITE PROMINENT. I DON'T KNOW HOW THEY FARE NOW, THOUGH.

BUT SEEING YOU BRINGS BACK MEMORIES. HOW IS YOUR FATHER? IS HE WELL?

ONE WOULD THINK THAT FOR SOMEONE WHO PRACTICALLY RAISED YOU FOR FOUR YEARS OF YOUR LIFE, I SHOULD HAVE THE OPPORTUNITY TO SEE YOU A LITTLE MORE OFTEN.

UM, YES. VERY WELL, THANK YOU.

012

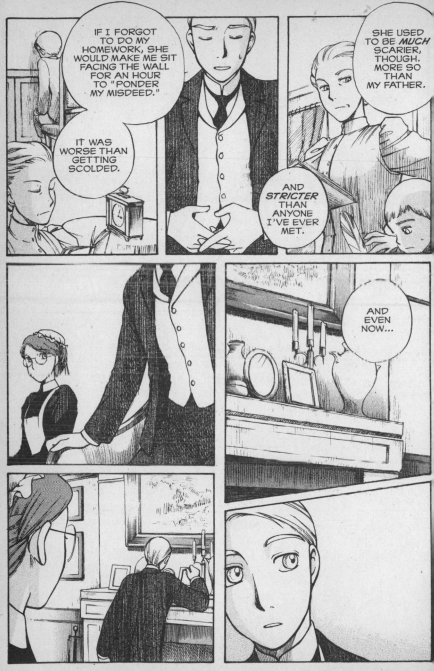

016

PERHAPS YOU'RE RIGHT. EVEN THOUGH I WAS CONSTANTLY ON THE RECEIVING END OF HER ANGER.

SHE PROBABLY THINKS OF YOU AS HER OWN SON.

IF SHE DECORATES THE MANTLEPIECE WITH YOUR PHOTO...

YES, I CAN IMAGINE. BUT THAT'S HER WAY.

IT WOULD BE NICE IF YOU COULD GET OVER YOUR SENSE OF UNEASE AROUND HER.

OH, UM...

...BY THE WAY...

QUITE.

018

...I SHALL SEE YOU AGAIN SOON.

VERY GOOD.

UM, WELL, THEN...

Chapter One:
The End

THE SYNDENHAM CRYSTAL PALACE WAS BUILT HERE, FOR THE GREAT EXPOSITION.

IN SOCIETY "OFF-SEASON," AS IT IS NOW, THIS IS A FINE PARK TO STROLL THROUGH.

AM I BORING YOU?

...AH. I'M SORRY, I'M HOGGING THE CONVERSATION.

GOOD.

OF COURSE, I'VE ONLY HEARD STORIES ABOUT THE EXPOSITION...

NOT AT ALL.

NO, NO.

PLEASE, CONTINUE.

...MAYBE WE SHOULD CHANGE THE SUBJECT.

...BUT THAT BIG ELM TREE BACK THERE? IT WAS SUPPOSED TO BE CUT DOWN. BUT...

A PACKAGE?

CHAPTER 2:
THE GLASSES

. . . . .

WHAT ARE YOU SAYING? YOU *ARE* YOUNG MASTER.

I am an adult, you know.

ISN'T IT ABOUT TIME YOU STOPPED REFERRING TO ME AS "YOUNG MASTER?"

SUPERB! IT'S ARRIVED SOONER THAN I EXPECTED!

HAVE YOU ORDERED SOMETHING, YOUNG MASTER?

TWIST THIS AROUND LIKE SO...

WHAT'S IT CALLED AGAIN? AN AERO-PLANE?

MM.

WELL, I'LL BE... THIS IS NICELY PUT TOGETHER FOR ITS SIZE.

EHEH HEH. SORRY!

YOUNG MASTER!!

You're faster on your feet than I give you credit for.

OH!

HYAAA!!

MY FATHER...

...WHICH MEANS I'M IN FOR A LONG TALK.

OH, YES. THE DELIVERY OF THE PACKAGE MADE ME FORGET TO TELL YOU...

...YOUR FATHER WOULD LIKE TO SEE YOU.

YOUNG MASTER!!

WHERE ARE YOU GOING?

FOR A LITTLE WALK.

BUT YOU CAN'T, YOUNG MASTER. YOUR FATHER IS EXPECTING YOU.

MAYBE I'LL TAKE A WALK TO SEE MISS EMMA.

I WISH I COULD JUST RUN INTO HER BY CHANCE...

...BUT WITH MY LUCK, THAT'LL NEVER...

She's too well-guarded...

NO, BAD IDEA.

035

. . . . .

CAREFUL YOU DON'T CUT YOUR HANDS.

...SOMETIMES EVEN AFTER YOU CLEAN THEM, THERE'S STILL DUST IN THE CORNERS, SO DO A MORE THOROUGH JOB FROM NOW ON.

...ABOUT THE STAIRS...

BY THE WAY...

YES, MA'AM.

LOOK. IT'S RIGHT *THERE.*

I WONDER WHOSE IT IS.

TSK! THAT DOG WANDERS INTO MY YARD, EASY AS YOU PLEASE.

WOOF!

WOOF!

. . .

WELL ...

DO THEY FIT?

TELL ME ...

ARE YOUR EYES *BAD?*

THEY MAY FEEL STRANGE UNTIL YOU GET USED TO THEM...

THE BIRDS...

THEY'RE FINE.

050

Chapter Two: The End

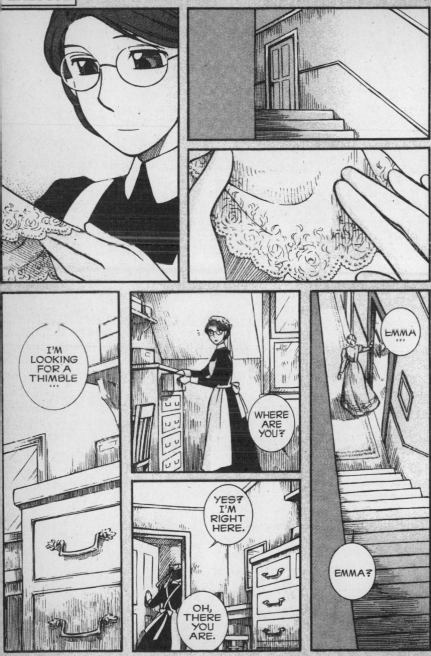

I'M LOOKING FOR A THIMBLE ...

WHERE ARE YOU?

YES? I'M RIGHT HERE.

OH, THERE YOU ARE.

EMMA ...

EMMA?

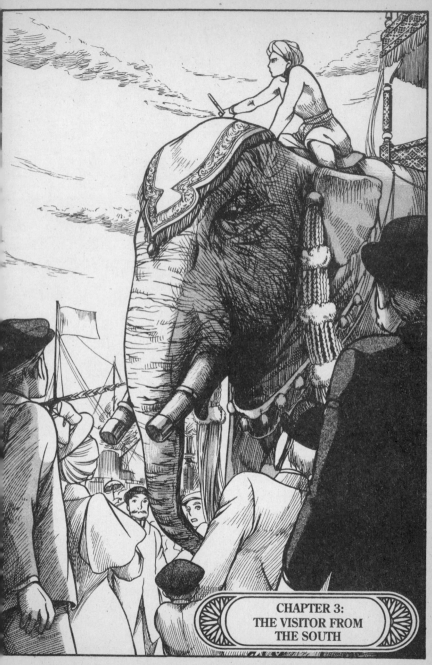

CHAPTER 3:
THE VISITOR FROM
THE SOUTH

THE ABOVE IS LAST MONTH'S SALES...

WHEN ARE THE GOODS DUE TO ARRIVE BY STEAMER?

...AND HERE IS THIS MONTH'S PURCHASING LIST.

FINE.

KA-CHA

TELL THEM TO GET IT HERE AS SOON AS POSSIBLE.

THEY SHOULD HAVE BEEN HERE BY NOW. I'LL INQUIRE ONCE AGAIN.

BRRRING

059

ELEPHANTS IN MY COURTYARD FOR ONE WEEK...

ONE THING...

ANYWAY, I SHALL ACCEPT YOUR HOSPITALITY FOR A MERE WEEK.

...ONE WEEK?!

FEAR NOT, I'VE BROUGHT ALONG MOST OF MY OWN NECESSITIES.

OH, YES! I'M TRAVELING INCOGNITO, SO NOT A WORD ABOUT MY VISIT TO ANYONE.

YOUR SERVANTS SHALL DO FINE.

LOADING THE ELEPHANTS UP WAS NO PROBLEM, BUT WE'LL NEED A FEW MORE HANDS TO HELP US UNLOAD THEM.

MASTER WILLIAM...

WELL, IT CAN'T BE HELPED, I SUPPOSE. HELP THEM WITH THEIR LUGGAGE.

"PRINCE HAKIM ATAWALLY, OF THE ATAWALLY ROYAL FAMILY OF INDIA, IS STAYING AT THE JONES ESTATE WHILST TRAVELING INCOGNITO IN LONDON..."

HMF...

YES. THE ATAWALLY FAMILY ALSO ENGAGES IN TRADE.

THEY MOST LIKELY SHARE A BUSINESS CONNECTION.

AND HE'S FROM... *INDIA?*

THAT FAMILY HAS MORE WORLDLY ACQUAINTANCES THAN ONE MIGHT THINK...

...THOUGH THE VERY IDEA OF TRAVELING "INCOGNITO" IS SHATTERED ONCE ITS PUBLISHED IN THE PAPERS.

OH, PLEASE!!

I WONDER IF THEY RIDE ELEPHANTS?

INDIA...

ON... ON AN ELE- PHANT ...?

ACTUALLY, NO ONE'S SUPPOSED TO RIDE THEM BUT ME, BUT YOU'RE A SPECIAL CASE!

EH?

MY COVER IS ALREADY BLOWN, SO WE MIGHT AS WELL GIVE THE PEOPLE SOMETHING TO LOOK AT!

সেসএ! LET'S RIDE!

WH...?

GULP

071

THIS IS HAKIM.

HE'S HOLIDAYING IN LONDON.

......

?

HELLO.

YES, MA'AM.

EMMA?

EMMA...

?

THANK YOU.

BE CAREFUL.

I'M SORRY TO HAVE DROPPED IN UNANNOUNCED.

GIVE MY REGARDS TO YOUR FATHER.

I'M HOPING FOR AN ANSWER BY AROUND THE NEXT DELIVERY.

NOT THAT I HAVE THE FAINTEST CHANCE, BUT IT'S FROM *ME*.

GOOD-BYE, FOR NOW.

CHAPTER 4: THE LOVE LETTERS

IT MEANS THAT THE MERCHANDISE YOU ORDERED IS READY AND HAS BEEN DELIVERED.

"WILBUR AND HOPKINS"...

WHAT DOES IT MEAN?

WILBUR & HOPKINS
LONDON, STREET. 48

THE GENTLEMAN IS WAITING FOR YOU IN THE PARLOR.

INDEED.

WELL. WHERE IS IT?

Buying so much these days, it slipped my mind.

I DON'T RECALL PLACING AN ORDER WITH THIS COMPANY.

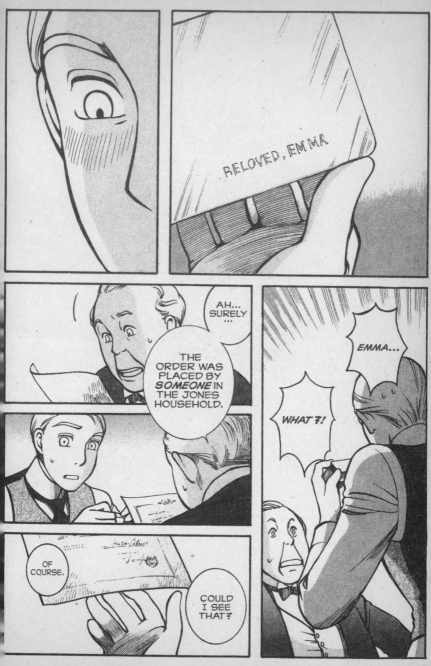

PLEASE, COME IN.

CLATTER

...I AM IN *LOVE* WITH YOU.

...WELL, TELLING YOU THAT IS ONE REASON I CAME HERE TODAY.

MAINLY, THOUGH, I JUST WANTED A CHANCE TO SEE YOU AGAIN.

EVEN IF IT'S FOR THE LAST TIME.

100

YES, MA'AM.

WELL, THAT'S ALL RIGHT. DO AS YOU LIKE.

AS LONG AS IT DOESN'T AFFECT YOUR WORK TOMORROW.

AND WHAT ABOUT YOU...

YOUNG MASTER?

Chapter Four: The End

IS THERE A MESSAGE?

YES, OF COURSE.

THIS IS ONE OF OUR MOST POPULAR ITEMS.

YES, THERE'S THIS FETCHING SHOPGIRL NAMED SARAH WHO WORKS AT LEYTON'S.

GOOD.

AND FOR *YOU* AS WELL.

IT'S A *PERFECT* PRESENT FOR THE LADIES.

"THERE'S A RESTAURANT ON ST. JAMES STREET...

...AT THE HOTEL MEDAILLE.

MY MESSAGE TO HER IS...

THANK YOU.

YES, I'LL GIVE HER YOUR MESSAGE.

I WOULD LIKE TO HAVE DINNER WITH YOU THERE."

THANK *YOU*, SIR.

...WOULD YOU PASS THAT ALONG?

CHAPTER 5:
THE PHOTOGRAPH

OH... I MUST HAVE DRIFTED OFF.

I HAD A DREAM.

A DREAM?

YES.

...BUT IT'S GONE NOW. I CAN'T REMEMBER.

I BELIEVE IT WAS ABOUT SOMETHING A *LONG* TIME AGO...

IT'S GETTING *CHILLY* IN HERE. LIGHT THE FIRE, WOULD YOU?

MY NAME IS KELLY STOWNAR.

YES, MA'AM.

I MARRIED WHEN I WAS 18. AT 20, I BECAME A WIDOW.

I HAVE NO CHILDREN.

NOW RETIRED, I LIVE WITH MY MAID, EMMA.

AFTER MY HUSBAND DIED, I WORKED AS A GOVERNESS FOR OVER 30 YEARS.

IF I HAVE ANY CONCERNS... WELL...

SHE'S A GOOD GIRL.

...THEY'RE ABOUT WHAT WILL HAPPEN TO HER AFTER I'M GONE.

IF SHE WOULD GET MARRIED, THAT WOULD PUT MY MIND AT EASE.

YES?

MMM...

SHE'S YOUNG, SHE'S BEAUTIFUL, SHE'S A HARD WORKER...IF SHE WERE JUST A TAD LESS MEEK, SHE COULD HAVE ANY NUMBER OF SUITORS...

...BUT THE THING ABOUT EMMA IS THAT SHE DOESN'T CARE A FIG ABOUT THAT.

I WONDER IF ANYTHING HAS HAPPENED BETWEEN THEM AFTER THAT DAY.

BUT WHAT ABOUT YOUNG MASTER JONES?

I HAD FORGOTTEN ABOUT HIM.

SHE HASN'T SWIFTLY REJECTED HIM LIKE ALL THE OTHERS, MEANING...SHE FINDS HIM SUITABLE, PERHAPS?

· · · · · · ·

I WISH THE YOUNG MASTER WOULD ACT MORE LIKE A RESPONSIBLE ADULT, BUT AGEWISE, THEY'RE PERFECT FOR EACH OTHER.

NO, MY ONLY WORRY WOULD BE ABOUT HIS FAMILY.

SINCE WHEN DID I BECOME SUCH A MEDDLESOME OLD WOMAN? IS IT BECAUSE OF MY AGE?

114

115

AS MY HOUSE IS BECOMING WATER-LOGGED, I WOULD HAZARD A GUESS THAT THE DOWNPIPE IS BUSTED!

HELLO, AL! IT'S ME!!

I EXPECT TO SEE YOU *HERE* IN FIVE MINUTES!!

CLICK

I NEED YOU TO REPAIR IT, SO LEAVE RIGHT THIS MINUTE!!

THE WAY THIS IS GOING, WE'LL BE KNEE-DEEP IN NO TIME!

TELL HER I'M NOT A RECEP-TIONIST.

...I'VE BEEN SUM-MONED.

YOU WOULDN'T LET TWO WOMEN MOVE ALL OF THIS BY THEMSELVES, WOULD YOU?

I'M SURE SHE WAS A HANDFUL FOR DOUG, TOO.

THAT KELLY'S BEEN MY SLAVE DRIVER SINCE *WAY* BACK.

HEAVE-HO!

BAM

118

...WELL, SURE. WE LIVED IN THE SAME NEIGBORHOOD.

DID YOU KNOW HER HUSBAND?

WHEN WE WERE BRATS, WE ALWAYS USED TO NICK APPLES FROM COVENT GARDEN, STUFF LIKE THAT...

SO YOU WERE...

NO, NEVER... ALL I KNOW IS THAT HER HUSBAND PASSED AWAY.

SHE DOESN'T TALK TO YOU ABOUT "OLD TIMES?"

HMPH.

WELL, I GUESS T'AIN'T A SUBJECT THAT'D BE MUCH FUN TO DREDGE UP.

WHAT'S THAT?

ER, I MEAN...

...FRIENDS WITH BOTH MY LADY AND HER *HUSBAND*?

...ACTUALLY, I WAS WONDERING WHERE THEY MET.

...REALLY?

THAT'S HOW IT WAS FOR EVERYONE BACK IN THE DAY.

OH, THE *USUAL* WAY. THE PARENTS' DECISION.

WELL, YOU WOULDN'T, BECAUSE KELLY IS SO STUBBORN.

I NEVER IMAGINED...

THREE MEETINGS AND THEN THE WEDDING IS THE WAY IT USUALLY WORKED.

121

122

SHE JUST ASKED ABOUT DOUG, SO I TOLD HER.

AL, YOU WERE TALKING TO EMMA BEFORE, WEREN'T YOU?

I HOPE YOU WEREN'T TELLING TALES OUT OF SCHOOL.

I SEE.

EMMA ASKED...?

I BELIEVE IT'S A NECK-LACE.

I THINK I COLLECTED ALL OF THE PIECES BUT...

WHAT IS *THAT?*

123

. . . . . .

...TO PUT IT BACK TOGETHER.

...I DON'T KNOW HOW...

. . . . . .

THE STRING MUST HAVE BROKEN.

UNLUCKY DAY.

YES, MA'AM.

AH, WELL. PUT IT AWAY AS IS.

THOROUGHLY.

WHEN IT RAINS, IT POURS.

WELL, YES, CERTAINLY...

NO, I FIND DURING AND AFTER THE RAIN TO BE QUITE UNPLEAS-ANT. TOO DAMP BY HALF.

IT FEELS SOMEHOW REFRESH-ING, DON'T YOU THINK?

NO, I DESPISE THE RAIN ITSELF. LIKE IT WHEN THE RAIN STOPS.

YOU LIKE THE RAIN?

SHALL I CHANGE THE BANDAGES, MADAM?

OH, YES. GO AHEAD.

WHAT DO YOU THINK OF YOUNG MASTER JONES?

TELL ME, EMMA...

DO YOU INTEND TO TURN *HIM* DOWN, TOO?

......

MMM, YES...

Actually, not much in this world seems to bother him...

HE'S UNUSUAL.

HIGH-BORN AND YET, IT DOESN'T BOTHER HIM AT ALL THAT I'M A MAID.

AND DO YOU *LOVE* HIM?

HE HASN'T GIVEN ME THE STANDARD "YES/NO" CHOICE AS THE OTHERS HAVE.

......

HE JUST SEEMS TO...TAKE PLEASURE IN *CONVERSING* WITH ME.

129

THE PHOTO WAS TAKEN RIGHT AFTER WE HAD GOTTEN MARRIED.

...E NEVER ...DREAM.

CURIOUS...

COME TO THINK OF IT...

PERHAPS HE CAME TO TELL ME TO GET A MOVE ON, TO BE BY HIS SIDE...

...I BELIEVE IT WAS *HE* WHO APPEARED IN THAT DREAM I HAD.

Chapter Five: The End

EH, IT'LL MAKE A NICE KEEPSAKE.

SO YOU TOOK A PICTURE, EH?

KELLY'S A BEAUTY, IN'T SHE?

WE HAD TO STAY STILL FOR THE LONGEST TIME.

DOES A MAN SAY THAT ABOUT HIS OWN WIFE?

MY SHOULDERS ARE STIFF.

SAY... AL, GO OUT AND BUY SOME MORE.

ASK DOUG HERE!

ME?

NOW LEAVE AT ONCE!

DOUG IS MY HUSBAND.

SLAVE DRIVER!

I CANNOT HAVE HIM RUNNING ERRANDS.

OH, DEAR. WE'RE OUT OF SUGAR.

131

ASHES TO ASHES, DUST TO DUST.

133

THE PHOTO WAS TAKEN RIGHT AFTER WE HAD GOTTEN MARRIED.

COME TO THINK OF IT...

...I BELIEVE IT WAS HE WHO APPEARED IN THAT DREAM I HAD.

PEOPLE SURROUND THEMSELVES WITH PHOTOS AND MEMENTOES OF THEIR LOST LOVED ONES...

PERHAPS HE CAME TO TELL ME TO GET A MOVE ON, TO BE BY HIS SIDE...

136

...

BY THE WAY, HAKIM, I'VE BEEN MEANING TO ASK YOU...

RIDE WHERE?!

OUTSIDE, OF COURSE, AS YOU SAID!

COME, LET US RIDE!!

EH?!

VRRRR

Well, good.

...

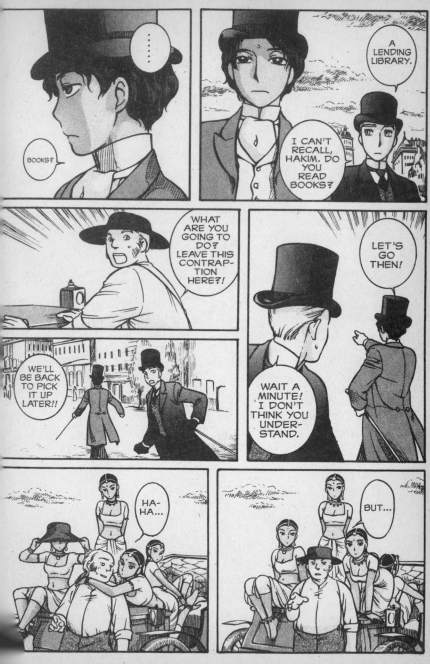

146

YOUR MEMBER-SHIP CARD, PLEASE.

THAT'S THREE BOOKS ALTOGE-THER.

LET ME SEE...

...IS MY LADY'S. I'M HERE AS HER PROXY.

EH?

BUT THIS NAME...

UMMM... KELLY STOWNAR...

I DIDN'T *THINK* SHE WAS THAT YOUNG.

AH, NOW I SEE.

148

153

154

AH! THAT'S...

...KELLY'S GIRL.

MM?

YOU'VE GOT EAGLE EYES.

WHERE?

SHE'S RUNNING. LORD, SHE'S YOUNG.

WHO SAID THAT, GOETHE?

...FOR THIS WORLD ALLOWS YOU NO MORE THAN A CUPFUL OF DREAMS. SO BE STINGY WITH YOUR TIME.. AND RUN.

OR SOMETHING LIKE THAT.

NO, ME.

RUN, RUN, YOUNG ONE...

"IF YOU STOP WALKING...

...IT MEANS YOUR DAY OF REST IS NEAR."

At the end of the 19th century, in England...

...the averaage life span was 50 years.

Chapter Six: The End

NO, I'M AFRAID THERE'S NONE OF THAT AROUND HERE.

SAYS HE'S LOOKING FOR OIL FOR HIS MOTORCAR.

WHAT'S THAT?

BUT I CAN'T THINK OF A SINGLE SHOP 'ROUND HERE THAT SELLS THAT KINDA STUFF.

MMM... I THOUGHT NOT.

HAHA! RAN OUT OF PETROL!

JUST GOES TO SHOW THAT EVEN ARISTOCRATS AREN'T STRANGERS TO FOOLISHNESS.

HE RAN OUT OF PETROL, SO HIS MOTORCAR'S STALLED.

OIL?

NOT FOR ME A YOUNG NOBLEMAN.

NOTHING. NOT IMPORTANT.

HUH?

FOOLISH ARISTOCRAT, HM...?

SOUNDS LIKE THAT "YOUNG MASTER" KELLY WAS TALKING ABOUT.

WELL, THERE'S NOTHING FOR IT, I'D BETTER LOOK FOR A CART.

GO RIGHT AHEAD.

TAKE CARE A' YOURSELF.

FRÜHLINGSSTIMMEN

Op.41

CHAPTER 7:
THE FATHER, RICHARD JONES

BUT SOON AS IT FLED, HE DREW A BEAD AND FIRED ONE SHOT!

BLAM!!

AND IT TOOK FIVE DOGS TO DRIVE IT OUT OF ITS HOLE.

HIS SKILL AS A HORSEMAN IS A GIVEN, BUT HE'S ALSO FIRST-RATE WITH RIFLES.

THERE ISN'T A FOX AROUND THAT HAS CAUGHT HIS EYE AND ESCAPED TO TELL ABOUT IT.

...MY MEN DO LOVE TO TALK ABOUT HUNTING.

DO YOU ENJOY LAMBS-GATE?

IT APPEARS YOU ARE BORING THE LADIES, OLD CHAP.

IT'S A MARVEL-OUS STORE.

BY THE WAY, DID YOU KNOW THAT A NEW STORE HAS OPENED O REGENT STREET

YES, I OFTEN HOLIDAY THERE IN THE SUMMER.

THEY USE FRENCH DESIGNERS.

WHY, YES! I SHOPPED THERE THE OTHER DAY.

162

THE INVITATIONS THAT YOU'VE DECLINED.

...RECENTLY, YOU'VE TURNED DOWN ALMOST ALL OF THE INVITATIONS YOU'VE GOTTEN.

I'VE HEARD FROM STEPHENS HERE THAT...

MY APOLOGIES, SIR.

EPHENS, HAVE ING TO ORRY R.

QUITE THE CONTRARY IT APPEARS THAT YOU HAD STEPHENS DO ALL THE DECLINING *FOR YOU.*

...TRUE.

PERHAPS IT'S BECAUSE YOU'RE YOUNG, BUT YOU LACK BASIC UNDER-STANDING OF THE *NECESSITY* OF SOCIAL CONTACTS.

...I'M SORRY. THERE WERE JUST SO MANY OF THEM...

BECAUSE OF OUR FORTUNE?

WELL, THAT, TOO.

WITHOUT ANY CLAIM TO NOBILITY, THE JONES FAMILY, A FAMILY OF MERCHANTS, IS ACCEPTABLE AMONG THE GENTRY AS ONE OF ITS OWN.

WHY DO YOU SUPPOSE THAT IS?

AND THE BEST PLACE TO CLEARLY EXPRESS THESE ELEMENTS...

...IS IN FASHIONABLE SOCIETY.

BUT THERE ARE THREE ELEMENTS EVEN MORE CRITICAL THAN THAT.

NAMELY, GRACE, INTELLECT AND DECORUM.

FIRST FASHIONABLE SOCIETY IS MADE UP OF THE ARISTOCRACY.

STRICTLY SPEAKING, YOU SHOULD ACCEPT *EVERY* INVITATION YOU RECEIVE.

THIS, TOO, IS BUSINESS.

..WITH HAKIM ..GITING ...

BUT...

SURELY, EVEN YOU REALIZE THAT MUCH.

WITH HIS NEW FACE AND APPARENT ABILITY TO STAND OUT IN A CROWD, HE'S GOT ALL THE LADIES' TOUNGUES WAGGING. SPECULATION IS RUNNING RAMPANT AS TO HIS INDENTITY.

HUH. SO HE'S *YOUR* FRIEND, IS HE?

"TO THE MANOR BORN."

THIS SETTING IS HIS FORTE.

WELL, BE AS IT THAT AS IT MAY, IT DOES US NO GOOD STANDING LIKE STATUES.

HIS FORTE, EH?

...IS IT NOT?

OURS IS TO MEET, GREET, MAKE THE ROUNDS, DANCE A WALTZ OR TWO...

SO I'VE BEEN ...LD...

IT'S NOT ESPECIALLY UP MY ALLEY.

MR. WILLIAM JONES?

THEN WHY BOTHER COMING?

...I FIND IT ALL VERY TIRESOME.

...BUT TO BE PERFECTLY HONEST...

GOOD EVENING.

IT'S BEEN TOO LONG MADAM.

OH, YOU'RE HERE TOO, ROBERT.

FAR TOO LONG.

ARE YOUR FATHER AND MOTHER WELL?

YES, I WOULD VENTURE TO SAY THEY'RE STILL ENJOYING GOOD HEALTH AND CLEVER MINDS.

NO, NO. NOTHING LIKE *THAT*...

I HADN'T SEEN YOU FOR SO LONG, I THOUGHT PERHAPS YOU HAD TAKEN ILL...

170

172

174

WELL, ACTUALLY, I DIDN'T HEAR IT STRAIGHT FROM THE SOURCE, SO...

IT'S *ABSURD!* WHY DIDN'T YOU INFORM ME OF SUCH IMPORTANT NEWS?

WHETHER THE INFORMATION COMES FIRST-HAND OR FROM THE GRAPEVINE, WHEN YOUR FORMER TEACHER IS ILL IN BED...

...YOU PAY HER A VISIT.

RATTLE RATTLE

WILLIAM, YOU SIMPLY MUST BECOME MORE AWARE OF THE CONCEPT OF COURTESY.

YES, BUT I DON'T SEE WHY *YOU* HAVE TO GO AS WELL.

I'VE BEEN MEANING TO VISIT ANYWAY, SO THIS COMES AS PERFECT TIMING.

IT TOOK OVER *TEN YEARS* OF MY HARANGUING BEFORE YOU FINALLY SAW TO CALL O... YOUR TEACH...

RATTLE RATTLE

PLEASE, COME IN.

IT'S BEEN A LONG TIME, MR. JONES.

YOU HAVEN'T CHANGED A BIT.

HOW *KIND* OF YOU TO COME.

FORGIVE ME FOR NOT GETTING UP.

AND YOU LOOK IN MUCH BETTER SPIRITS THAN I IMAGINED.

OH, I'VE ONLY INJURED MY LEG.

IT'S NOTHING *SERIOUS.*

THAT'S QUITE ALL RIGHT, MRS. STOWNAR.

THAT'S VERY GRACIOUS OF YOU TO SAY SO.

...OH, NO. THAT'S NOT TRUE. HE WAS A GOOD STUDENT.

IT MAY BE HIS NATURAL DISPOSITION, BUT HE'S ALWAYS BEEN A TAD, SHALL WE SAY, UNFOCUSED.

HE WAS JUST SOMEWHAT EASILY DISTRACTED.

RIBIT

PERHAPS IT'S JUST HIS AGE.

IF I'VE SAID IT ON I'VE SAID A HUND TIMES THE BOY LACKS AWAR

178

179

180

HAVE YOU *ANOTHER* GIRL IN MIND?

......

I ASSUME SHE IS A PROPER LADY, SUITABLE TO MARRY INTO THE JONES FAMILY?

......

I...

I...

THAT YOUR PERSONAL FEELINGS FOR THE WOMAN ARE IMPORTANT IS BEYOND DISPUTE. HOWEVER...

...MARRIAGE BETWEEN TWO PEOPLE FROM THE SAME *COUNTRY* IS TO BE DESIRED.

OH, SHE'S NOT A FOREIGNER.

EMMA...

Chapter 7: The End

AFTERWORD MANGA

THEME

GENTLEMAN'S FANCY:
MAIDS IN BLACK

THANK YOU VERY MUCH FOR BUYING AND/OR READING THIS, THE FIRST VOLUME OF ""EMMA!"

I love 'em!

DO YOU LIKE MAIDS? DO YOU LIKE ENGLAND?

HELLO, NICE TO MEET YOU! I'M KAORU MORI, THE CREATOR OF "EMMA."

EMMA

ABOUT OUR PROTAGONIST, SHE'S A MAID WHO'S QUIET BEAUTIFUL, WEARS GLASSES, IS SHY...

Uwaaa!

...AND IS CONSTANTLY TWISTING IN EMBARRASSMENT, BUT WRITING AND DRAWING THIS IS FUN FOR ME, SO POOR EMMA!

THERE'S NO WAY I CAN DISGUISE OR EXCUSE MY OBVIOUS MANIA FOR ALL THINGS ENGLISH.

"EMMA," WHICH IS MY FIRST SERIALIZED MANGA, BY THE WAY, IS THE STORY OF A MAID IN ENGLAND AT THE END OF THE 19TH CENTURY.

Stereotypes of England

Holmes never had a moustache.

NO ONE GETS THE PURPOSE OF THE INDIAN GIRLS.

Actually, I just like this kind of character.

OUR FORMER TEACHER, KELLY, LOOKS SO DIFFERENT IN CHAPTERS 1 AND 7 THAT IT LOOKS LIKE SHE GOT COSMETIC SURGERY SOMEWHERE IN BETWEEN.

How rude!

AS FOR THE REST, WE'VE GOT WHATSIS-NAME, THE EXHAUSTING RICH KID HERE, BUT ACTUALLY, HE'S THE EASIEST TO DRAW.

WILLIAM JONES

I GUESS HE MAKES ME EXHAUSTED BECAUSE OF HIS EXASPERATING CHARACTER.

...THE MOST **IMPORTANT THING OF ALL...**

IT'S IMPORTANT!!

IMPORTANT!!

...TANT!!

EMMA EMBARRA FACE I

SORRY.

STILL, I'VE GOT ALL KINDS OF IDEAS THAT'LL PROBABLY GET JAMMED INTO VOLUME 2.

DADDY

...BUT I THINK THE STORY IS STARTING TO MOVE FORWARD NOW.

AND SO I PRETTY MUCH GET TO DO WHAT I WANT KELLY HAS AN ACCIDENT, DADDY APPEARS...

A FAN →

Poo-poo-pee-doo ♡

MONROE

I BOUGHT THE MARILYN MONROE DVD BOXED SET AND HAVE BEEN WATCHING LIKE A MONKEY EVERY SINGLE DAY.

IF FATE ALLOWS, LET'S MEE AGAIN IN VOLUME

SEE YOU THEN!

Ciao ♡

WILL EMMA AND WILLIAM'S RELATIONSHIP SURVIVE? FIND OUT IN DECEMBER.

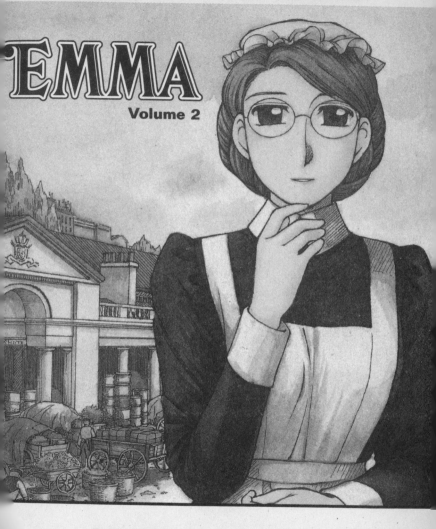

EMMA

Volume 2

By Kaoru Mori. After Emma and William's first real date, things seem to be going in a positive direction for them. But the leisurely pace of their growing relationship ends when tragedy strikes at home, forcing Emma to leave the house she shared with Mrs. Stownar. Meanwhile, when the rest of William's brothers and sisters show up, they discover their brother's budding relationship and try to bring it to a screeching halt.

Welcome to Emma's World

In Victorian London, as the end of the 19th century approached, picking yourself up by your own bootstraps and lifting yourself out of poverty wasn't really an option. Class defined your future, not your own ambition—sadly, it was even worse for women. For a girl not born into the upper classes and abandoned at an early age, prospects for the future were especially grim.

If you were that girl, what would happen if a kind-hearted woman—former governess to an aristocratic family—took you in? If she decided to take care of you and train you to become a proper British maid? A li[ ] of servitude may not seem glamorous to those of us living in today's world, but it would have been a great stroke of luck for someone trapped by poverty, someone whose other choices were the poorhouse or the slu[ ] of London. Of course, the lucky person in our story is Emma, the star of this series.

The Woman Behind EMMA

EMMA is the creation of Kaoru Mori, a relatively young mangaka (she's under 30) who harbors a real love [ ] all things British, but particularly for the England of the Victorian era. It's hard to explain what attracts certain people to different cultures and time periods that are alien and far-removed from their own. But whatever the reason, Ms. Kaoru's passion comes through on every page.

She has carefully researched her material, and every illustration is meticulously drawn to create as accurat[ ] depiction of London circa 1885 as possible. In fact, she even brought in an historical consultant to assure [ ] series' accuracy. The kind of realistic art direction seen in the pages of EMMA is something that people are perhaps more accustomed to experiencing in cinema rather than comics. The total effect makes you feel th[ ] you are there with the characters in the world she has created (or recreated, as the case might be). There is nothing supernatural or fantasy-related about the adventures of EMMA. It's simply a lovingly rendered speculation on what it might have been like to live in London as a maid in that bygone era.

Ms. Kaoru has been publishing the serialized adventures of Emma in a Japanese monthly anthology called *Comic Beam* (Enterbrain) since 2002. In that short time, the series has captured an intensely loyal followi[ ] and a highly praised anime series was spun out from this manga. (As of this writing, the series is unavaila[ ] in America.) EMMA created something of a phenomenon in Japan and is said to have spawned an interest [ ] English maid "cosplay" with fans dressing up in the attire of the series. We hope that we can help spread t[ ] kind of enthusiastic following to America as well.

EMMA just recently concluded its run in Japan in early 2006. We at CMX are excited to be presenting the [ ] collected, translated versions of EMMA in their entirety and un-retouched. We hope you will enjoy your journey back through time, as you follow the adventures of Emma, William, Kelly Stownar and all the wonderful, three-dimensional characters from the mind of master storyteller Kaoru Mori.

Jim Chadwick

Jim Chadwick
CMX Editor

CHECK OUT THIS TITLE!

OYAYUBIHIME — Volume 2 — INFINITY

By Toru Fujieda. Kanoko and friends have begun searching for a person with a butterfly-shaped birthmark on her thumb — the sign of a time-spanning connection from a past life — to find Tsubame's supposed true love. Who was this person, and what's she like now? But Tsubame might not be ready to give up on Kanoko just yet. He's got to persuade her that love is more important than fate.

BIHIME INFINITY (OYAYUBIHIME ∞) Vol. 2 © 2004 Toru Fujieda/Akitashoten.